C1

D1256256

PASSPORT TO MEXICO

Carmen Irizarry

Revised Edition

Franklin Watts

New York/Chicago/London/Toronto/Sydney

Copyright ©1987, Second Edition 1994 Franklin Watts

Franklin Watts
95 Madison Avenue
New York, NY 10016

Library of Congress Cataloging-in-Publication Data
Irizarry, Carmen.
    Passport to Mexico / Carmen Irizarry. – Rev. ed.
      p.   cm. – (Passport to)
    Includes Index.
    Summary: Introduces the geography, industry, natural
resources, and people of Mexico.
    ISBN 0-531-14322-8
    1. Mexico – Juvenile literature.   [1. Mexico.]   I. Title.
II. Series.
    F1208.5.I75   1994   93-46692
    972.08′35 – dc20   CIP AC

Editor: Lynne Williams
Design: Edward Kinsey
Illustration: Hayward Art Group
Consultant: Keith Lye

Photographs: Tony and Marion Morrison,
ZEFA, Tony Hutchings, Mexicolore, Bridgeman
Art Library, BBC Hulton Picture Library, NASA,
Robert Harding Picture Library, Hutchison
Library, Mexican Embassy, Televisa s.a. de c.v.

Front cover: ZEFA; inset: James Davis Travel
Photography

Phototypeset by Keyspools Limited
Color reproduction by Hongkong Graphic Arts
Printed in Belgium

Contents

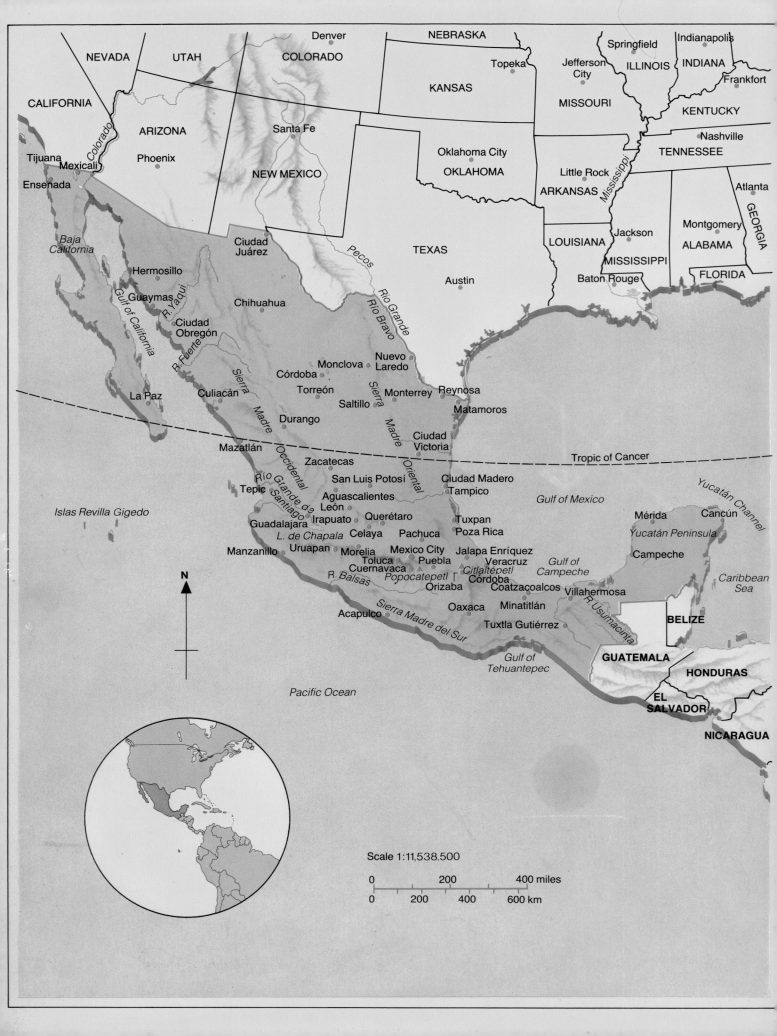

Introduction

Mexico occupies a unique position in North America. Its people and culture have strong ties with the countries of Latin America to the south. But it also has strong historical and economic links with the United States to the north. Thus Mexico bridges two vast and contrasting civilizations.

Mexico is a fascinating blend of Indian and Spanish cultures. This mixture is reflected in the country's ancient traditions, its customs, beliefs and ways of life. Yet Mexico is changing fast. Its people are eager for economic and social progress.

In the 1970s, Mexico's rich oil reserves provided income to develop the economy. But when the demand for oil fell in the early 1980s, Mexico faced economic problems. In the late 1980s, it set about rebuilding its economy. A major development in 1993 was the signing of the North American Free Trade Agreement (NAFTA), aimed at creating a common market with Canada and the United States.

Above: Remains of ancient Indian civilizations are found in many parts of Mexico. This is a Mayan Temple at Palenque.

Below: New offices, apartments and hotels to the north of Mexico City.

The land

Mexico is a long, narrow country bordered by the Pacific Ocean to the west, and the Gulf of Mexico and the Caribbean Sea to the east. Extending down the west coast is a long peninsula known as Baja California. In the southern region another great landmass – the Yucatán Peninsula – thrusts far into the Gulf of Mexico.

The country's landscape is extremely varied. It includes deserts, grasslands, snow-capped mountains and humid tropical forests. In the north, where the land is arid or semi-arid, temperatures can range from very hot to bitter cold. The southern coastlands, in contrast, have a sub-tropical or tropical climate and lush vegetation. In the south, too, there is a rainy season, between May and October.

The Pacific coastal plains are very arid in the north and give way to tropical, humid conditions in the south. The Yucatán and the Gulf Coast form the largest lowland area in Mexico. Its northern parts are dry while others are covered by swamps and lagoons.

Above: Pine forests cover the slopes of the Sierra Madre Occidental mountain range, near Toluca, in central Mexico.

Left: Oaxaca in southern Mexico lies at an altitude of 1,500 m (4,921 ft) above sea level. It is not easy for farmers to grow crops in this arid land.

Left: Acapulco, on the Pacific coast, has a humid tropical climate.

Below: Tropical plants, such as bananas, grow in profusion along river valleys,as here in Jalisco State.

Altitude, however, is the dominant physical feature in Mexico. Beginning south of Mexico City, and running north like the arms of a letter Y, are two great mountain chains – the Sierra Madre Occidental and the Sierra Madre Oriental. Among their peaks are Orizaba (Citlatépetl), the country's highest point, and the famous Popacatépetl, whose Indian name means "Smoking Mountain". Both are dormant volcanoes over 5,000 m (16,500 ft) high. The Southern Highlands, or Sierra Madre del Sur, extend from Mexico City along the Pacific coast.

The largest and most important feature of Mexico is, however, the Central Plateau which extends from the United States border to south of Mexico City. It rises to altitudes between 1,000 and 2,000 m (3,300 and 6,600 ft). The Plateau covers over half of Mexico and contains most of the major cities. Its fertile land and equable climate are able provide much of Mexico's food requirements.

The people

Modern Mexico is the product of two contrasting civilizations, the Indians and the Spanish. These two cultures have blended to form a unique way of life.

The earliest people in Mexico were the descendants of people who entered North America from Asia around 20,000 years ago. As these people spread south, they formed distinct groups and built civilizations. For example, the Mayas of Mexico left exquisite sculptures and temples. They also made many scientific discoveries. Other early empires in Mexico included the Toltec, Zapotec and Mixtec.

When the Spaniards reached Mexico in 1519, the most powerful people were the Aztecs. In two years, the Spaniards defeated the Aztec empire and Mexico became a colony of Spain called *New Spain*. Over the years, the Spaniards and local people intermarried. Today, nearly 80 per cent of the population is of mixed ancestry. They are called *mestizos*.

Above: Girls about to take their First Communion. The Catholic faith plays a very important part in Mexican life.

Below: Any crowd of people will illustrate the mixture of local people and Spaniards that form the Mexican population.

Above: A street trader selling fruit pieces.

Below: Businessmen in Mexico City.

Above: A seller of models made from spare parts.

Below: A stone mason. His forebears carved temples.

Mexico's population growth has been spectacular since the 1910 Revolution. At that time there were 15 million people. Today there are more than 80 million. A high death rate was reduced by the introduction of health and sanitation services. Until the early 1970s the population was increasing faster than in any other major country, and doubling every 20 years. This huge increase has led to job shortages and a drain on schools, hospitals and other facilities.

Although Mexican culture is a mixture of the Spanish and Indian civilizations, the people themselves are mainly Indian in origin. Over 50 local dialects are spoken. But Spanish is the official language and most people speak it. Many people speak both Spanish and at least one of the local languages.

The majority of Mexicans are Roman Catholics as a result of the Spanish influence. The great Christian festivals are celebrated with much pageantry and ritual by a large part of the population.

Above: Children with their paintings.

Below: The bass player of a *mariachi* group.

Where people live

The most densely populated parts of Mexico are on the southern plains of the fertile Central Plateau. The most sparsely inhabited regions are the country's two peninsulas – Baja California to the north and the Yucatán in the southeast.

Since the 1950s there has been a large-scale migration from the rural areas to the towns and cities. The prospects of a better job and better living conditions are the main reasons for this drift. Generally improved transportation and communications have also made migration easier. By 1991, 73 percent of the people lived in cities and towns, with the remaining 27 percent in rural settlements.

Today about 45 percent of the population live in cities with more than a million people, namely Mexico City, Guadalajara, Monterrey and Puebla. But Mexico City has about five times as many people as Guadalajara.

Above: A remote Indian village in southern Mexico. Many people have left such places to seek work in the cities.

Left: Taxco, southwest of Mexico City, was founded as a silver-mining town by the Spanish in the 16th century.

The spectacular growth of the cities has caused many problems. As the numbers grew, housing and municipal services began to break down. Like many other urban areas in the developing world, Mexico City is now ringed by low-grade housing where newcomers live while they look for work. This has led to the growth of large, unhealthy slums.

Many people still live in medium- to large-sized towns and provincial capitals. The colonial architecture of these towns, with their elegant plazas (squares), is often outstanding – stylish, solid and usually well built.

Such towns have also grown in recent years, and many new buildings have been constructed. Their inhabitants are fortunate that these towns usually lack the unhealthy conditions, pollution and overcrowding of the large cities. They are mostly well laid out, and their people lead a less hectic way of life. Town dwellers may be poorer than those who work in the large cities, but their lifestyles are generally considered to be more pleasant.

Above: Cities have grown up around Mexico's many sea-ports. This is Acapulco on the Pacific coast.

Below: A modern development which houses prosperous workers from Mexico City.

Mexico City

Mexico City is the capital of Mexico, the world's largest city and most ancient settlement in the Americas. It is built on the site of a drained lake where the Aztecs settled in the 14th century and built their capital, Tenochtitlán.

The city was destroyed in 1521 by the conquering Spaniards, who immediately began reconstruction around a great new square called the Zócalo. The Zócalo is still the heart of the old city. On one side of it is the cathedral, and on another is the National Palace, the seat of Mexican government. This section of the old city, with its grid-like layout, palaces and mansions, is the heart of the modern capital.

Mexico City has many famous landmarks and monuments commemorating Mexico's history. It also has one of the tallest buildings in the Americas, the 44-story Latin-American Tower. The city's main thoroughfare is the eight-lane highway, the Paseo de la Reforma. There is also a subway system, opened in 1969.

Above: Dominating the city is the Latin American tower which is 181 m (595 ft) high.

Below: Some of Mexico City's landmarks. They reflect centuries of Indian and Spanish civilization.

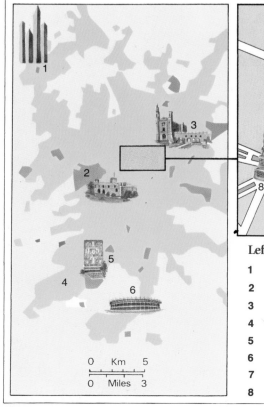

Left: Greater Mexico City

1   Satellite town
2   Chapultepec Park and Castle
3   Square of the Three Cultures
4   Olympic Stadium
5   University City
6   Aztec Stadium
7   Revolution Monument
8   Cuauhtemoc Monument

Above: Central Mexico City

9   Christopher Columbus Monument
10   Palace of Fine Arts
11   Latin-American Tower
12   Cathedral
13   Zocalo (Constitution Square)
14   National Palace
15   Colegio De Las Vizcainas

0   Km   5
0   Miles   3

Mexico City is the country's most important industrial base. Served by efficient road, rail and air links, it has a huge concentration of industries, including oil refining, textiles and clothing manufacture, and food processing. Half of the electricity generated in Mexico is used by these industries, which also employ 60 per cent of the city's total workforce. Tourism is also one of the major contributors to the city's economy.

In education and culture, Mexico City is equally important. The world-famous Palace of Fine Arts and the Museum of Anthropology are located here. The city also has nearly a quarter of Mexico's schools, as well as a vast university.

The rapid growth of its population is the city's greatest social problem, for there is much overcrowding. The city also suffers greatly from air pollution. The surrounding mountains unfortunately help to trap the fumes from factories and cars.

Above: Mexico City sprawls over a vast area. In the foreground is the splendid Palace of Fine Arts.

Below: A disastrous earthquake in 1985 brought down many buildings in the city, causing great loss of life.

Fact file: land and population

Key facts

Location: Mexico lies roughly between latitudes 33° and 15° North, and straddles the Tropic of Cancer. It is the third largest country in Latin America, and is bounded by the United States to the north and by Guatemala and Belize to the south.

Main parts: Mexico is divided into 31 states, and one federal district, Mexico City. Mexico includes two large peninsulas: Baja California in the northwest (758 miles/1,220 km long); and in the south, the Yucatán Peninsula.

Area: 761,605 sq miles (1,972,547 sq km).

Population: 89,000,000 (1992 estimate)

Capital: Mexico City

Major cities: with 1990 census populations:
Mexico City 13,636,000; total urban area, over 19,000,000
Guadalajara 2,847,000
Monterrey 2,522,000
Puebla 1,055,000
Léon 872,000
Ciudad Juárez 798,000
Tijuana 743,000
Mexicali 602,000
Culiacán 602,000
Acapulco 592,000
Mérida 557,000
Chihuahua 530,000
San Luis Potosi 526,000

Language: Spanish is the official language. Native languages are also spoken, including Maya, Mixtec, Náhuatl, Otomí and Zapotec.

Highest point: Orizaba (Citlaltépetl), an extinct, snow-capped volcano, southeast of Mexico City, 18,700 ft (5,700 m) above sea-level. It is North America's third highest peak.

Longest river: The Rio Bravo (Rio Grande in the United States). The river's total length is 1,880 miles (3,925 km), of which about 1,305 miles (2,100 km) form part of Mexico's northeastern border with the States. **Largest lake:** Lake Chapala, in the state of Jalisco, measures 53 miles (86 km) in length by 16 miles (25 km) at its widest.

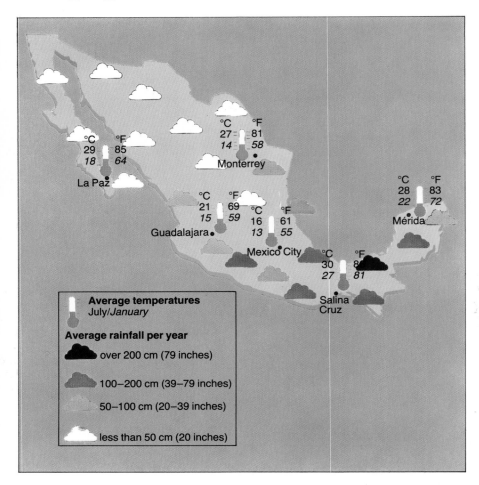

Average temperatures
July/*January*

Average rainfall per year

over 200 cm (79 inches)

100–200 cm (39–79 inches)

50–100 cm (20–39 inches)

less than 50 cm (20 inches)

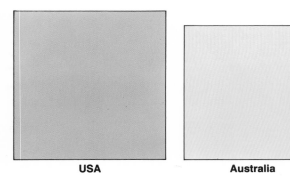

USA   Australia   Mexico   UK

△ **A land area comparison**
Mexico's 1,972,547 sq km (761,605 sq m) of territory make it a small country in comparison with the US, which has 9,370,000 sq km (3,600,000 sq m), or Australia with 7,650,000 sq km (2,470,000 sq m). But Mexico is far larger than many European countries. Britain, for example, has a land area of only 229,979 sq km (88,759 sq m) and is therefore eight times smaller than Mexico.

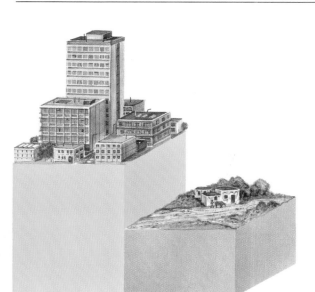

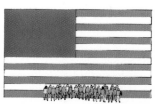

Australia 5 per sq mi (2 per sq km)

United States 70 per sq mi (27 per sq km)

Mexico 116 per sq mi (43 per sq km)

United Kingdom 614 per sq mi (234 per sq km)

Cities and towns 73% **Country 27%**

△**Where people live**
Cities and towns account for seven-tenths of Mexico's population. Both Baja California and the Yucatán peninsula are thinly populated.

△ **A population density comparison**
Mexico's population has increased greatly in recent years. But worldwide it is still rated as medium-low. There is a very unequal distribution between rural areas and the crowded, ever-expanding cities.

▷ **Major population centers**
Most people live on the Central Plateau. The areas in and round the larger ports also have substantial populations.

Legend:
- Major cities
- Main routeways
- Main ports

Tijuana, Mexicali, Cuidad Juárez, Chihuahua, Guaymas, Culiacán, Monterrey, San Luis Potosí, Tampico, Mérida, Mazatlán, Mexico City, León, Veracruz, Coatzacoalcos, Guadalajara, Puebla, Manzanillo, Lázaro Cárdenas, Acapulco, Salina Cruz, Puerto Madero

Home life

Above: A traditional house in a small village in central Mexico.

Below: A birthday provides the occasion for a family gathering near Veracruz.

The Mexican's home may be a modern urban apartment, a simple village dwelling, or a shanty on the edge of an industrial town. It may even be a mansion situated in an elegant quarter of Mexico City. Whatever its size or style, the house usually shelters a large and close-knit family.

In Mexico the average household has between five and six members. Many households include several generations. The grandparents share in the education of the young as much as the father and mother. The grandparents are left to look after the house and children if both parents go out to work.

Grown-up, unmarried children – especially girls – almost always live at home. Girls continue to share in the running of the household even if they have an outside job. When they marry some may move in with their in-laws. Close contact is the main rule of family life in Mexico.

Left: A living room with simple and practical furniture. There is a radio and record player, but no television.

Below: This family, living on the outskirts of Mexico City, is a typical example of the modern urban family.

It is almost always the women – either female members of the family, or a maid if there is one – who do the cooking and cleaning in a Mexican household. Cooking is usually elaborate, because mealtimes are regarded as important family occasions. For this reason the family home, however small, will generally have a proper dining room where old and young can sit down together. Bedrooms are nearly always shared, too, regardless of the social and economic standing of the family.

After the evening meal, the family will usually listen to the radio or gather round the television set. Throughout the year there are special celebrations to enjoy. Frequent national holidays herald parades and fireworks. Weddings and christenings bring gatherings of friends and relations which are followed by large, lavish parties. Mexicans love music and dancing, and spare no expense when a member of the family has reason to celebrate. Old or young, married or single, most Mexicans think, live and enjoy themselves as a family unit.

Shops and shopping

Most visitors to Mexico are immediately impressed by the vivid colours of goods on sale in the shops. Among the brightest are traditional blankets and shawls, hand-painted figurines, shiny red chilies and gleaming copperware.

In villages or rural areas trading often takes place at an outdoor market, or *tiangui*. The *tiangui* consists of a length of canvas on which the goods are laid, with a second piece hoisted above to make a roof. There are no fixed prices at *tianguis*, everyone haggles. The general bustle at outdoor markets is sometimes accompanied by lively music provided by local bands.

Most towns also have indoor markets housed in large, airy halls which were built at the beginning of the century or even earlier. Large numbers of street vendors can be seen in most cities. They sell almost anything from pet animals to toys and chinaware.

Above: In rural areas many people bring their goods to sell in open-air markets.

Below: Large indoor markets are common in every town and city. They sell a vast range of goods.

Small shops and stalls are found throughout Mexico. Handicraft dealers sell local pottery, silverwork and woven baskets, while the local grocery store will have shelves laden with food, especially herbs and spices.

Shopping in Mexico is often a social activity, as in many other countries. While shopping many people catch up on the local news and gossip. Local shops are open long hours and attract many people because of the personal attention given to customers. Supermarkets are also popular, especially with the more affluent families who are able to drive to the stores by car and so take advantage of cheaper bulk purchases.

Shopping in the large cities, such as Mexico City and Guadalajara, is often more impersonal, although the choice of goods is wider. As well as large markets, these cities have elegant boutiques and busy department stores which are open from 9.30 a.m. to 5.30 p.m. Their prices are too high for many people and they cater mostly for the affluent Mexican and the tourist trade.

Above: A local shop. Small grocers are very common and offer a wide range of foods.

Below: A shopping arcade in Guanajuato. It stocks modern merchandise and the latest fashions.

Cooking and eating

For Mexicans, meals are usually family occasions. Breakfast is always simple, consisting of coffee and bread or buns. Until recent times lunch was an elaborate meal. In small towns and in rural areas it is still the most important meal for most families. Dinner has, however, now become the main meal in large cities, where the distance between home and work may be considerable. The family can be together for a meal only in the evening.

Meals are usually accompanied by drinks such as fruit juices. Adults often have wine and beer, and sometimes the strong spirit known as *tequila*.

Mexico has given the world one of the most distinctive styles of cooking, and also a great many foodstuffs. Tomatoes, chocolate, vanilla and peanuts are just a few of the foods that originally came from Mexico and are now eaten throughout the world.

Above: The family have a modern kitchen. Most meals are eaten in a dining room.

Below: A family sits down to an outdoor meal. On the menu are chicken, *tortillas* and soft drinks.

Left: A snack can be obtained quickly at a *tortilla* bar. A wide range of fillings are available.

Below: *Chili con carne* is made with meat, beans, chili peppers, onions and spices. It is one of Mexico's most famous dishes.

Corn is the country's most important basic food. Since ancient times it has been used to make flat pancakes called *tortillas*. They are eaten like bread or made into a snack called a *taco* with different fillings. Beans are another important ingredient in the Mexican diet, either cooked and eaten on their own, or mixed with other ingredients. Beans are used in one of the most famous Mexican dishes – *chili con carne*.

Mexico has many other dishes that are not well known outside the country. One of these is *mole poblano*. It consists of chicken or turkey cooked in an elaborate sauce or *mole* made up of 30 to 40 ingredients including unsweetened chocolate, which gives the dish its brown color. Like many Mexican dishes, it is a blend of Indian and Spanish cooking.

Throughout Mexico *tortilla* and *taco* stands provide people with quick, freshly cooked meals at any time of the day. Most large towns and cities also have restaurants offering a variety of national and international dishes. These are popular and bustling places at lunchtime, when they are filled with workers and shoppers.

Pastimes and sports

Many of Mexico's pastimes and sports have their origins in Spain, but games from other countries, such as soccer, volleyball and tennis, are also popular.

Mexico played host to the world for the 1968 Olympic Games, and has been the venue for soccer's World Cup finals in 1970 and 1986. Soccer is the country's leading spectator sport. Matches held on local grounds or in huge stadiums such as the Azteca Stadium in Mexico City attract large, enthusiastic crowds. Other spectator sports with a large following include bullfighting introduced from Spain and baseball from the US. People also like the handball game known as *jai alai*, which originated in the Basque region of Spain.

Jogging is a popular activity, as in many countries, as a means to keep fit. For the less energetic, walking in the large city parks is a favourite pastime, often involving all the family.

Above: Most Mexicans are soccer enthusiasts. The national team, here playing England in 1983, has a devoted following.

Below: Bullfighting was introduced by the Spanish and is still popular, though soccer draws larger crowds.

Left: Mexican cowboys or *charros*, display their riding skill in rodeo-like *charreadas*.

Below: An Indian-style pageant before the church of Our Lady of Guadalupe in Mexico City.

Mexicans take fiestas and festivals very seriously, and celebrate them in style. Their national holidays include Christmas, Independence Day and Labor Day, but many other events, such as those marking Mexico's progress to democracy, are also celebrated. Most towns and villages also have their own local fiestas – usually in honor of their patron saint.

Christmas celebrations are extremely elaborate. On of the highlights for the children is the breaking up of the *piñata*. This is the name given to a brightly painted bag full of toys which is hung from the ceiling. The children are given poles which they use to break open the bag – hoping to bring down the shower of gifts.

At holiday time, many Mexican families like to attend *charreadas*. At these typical Mexican events, horsemen display riding, lassoing and other skills. The *charreadas* derive their name from the traditional costume of the riders, which is similar to that still worn by villagers of the province of Salamanca in Spain at their various fiestas.

News and broadcasting

Mexico has 390 newspapers, representing all shades of political opinion. The press enjoys great freedom of expression and debates national and international issues in a lively and forthright manner.

The total circulation of newspapers is more than 11 million copies. The main national newspapers are published in Mexico City. Those with large circulations include *Esto, Excélsior, El Heraldo de México, Novedades, Ovaciones* and *La Prensa.*

Other means of mass communication have also expanded greatly. For example, the country now has more than 1,000 radio broadcasting stations, most of which are commercial. The total number of radio receivers is about 16 million, or five persons per radio.

Movies are a popular form of entertainment in Mexico, with annual attendances of around 350 million. More films are made in Mexico than in any other Latin American nation.

Above: Mexicans are avid newspaper readers and have a free and open press.

Right: A huge range of publications are available, both produced in Mexico and imported. Among the most popular are fashion and sports magazines.

Left: Mexican Television (Televisa) filming an Indian festival in Mexico City.

Below: Jacobo Zabludovsky, a popular television news presenter.

Bottom: Veronica Castro, a TV star of entertainment and soap operas.

Television is becoming increasingly popular and by the mid-1980s more than 70 percent of homes had a television receiver. The national television network, *Televisa*, has its studios in Mexico City.

Throughout the country there are more than 200 television stations, of which eight are devoted exclusively to educational and cultural broadcasts. It is also possible to watch programs beamed directly from other countries, notably the United States.

Book publishing is a very dynamic sector of Mexico's communication industry. The first printing press in the New World was used in Mexico City in 1539, and books have been an important aspect of Mexican culture ever since. Until the 1930s, Spanish publishers exported books to Latin America in large numbers. The Spanish Civil War interrupted this trade. Mexico stepped in to fill the gap, and it has since then remained a leader in the field. At present, about 3,500 titles are published in Mexico each year. Most are in Spanish and go to markets on both sides of the Atlantic.

Fact file: home life and leisure

Key facts

Population composition: People under 15 years of age make up 37.6 percent of the population; people between 15 and 65 make up 60 percent; and people over 65 make up 2.4 percent.

Average life expectancy: 70 years (1991), as compared with 55 years in 1960. (By comparison, people in the United States live, on average, 76 years, while people in India live for 60 years.) Women make up 50.9 percent of the population. On average, women live to an age of 73 years, six years more than men.

Rate of population increase: Between 1970 and 1980, the population of Mexico increased at a rate of 2.9 percent per year. Between 1980 and 1991, it was 2.0 percent per year. An average yearly rate of 1.9 percent per year is forecast for the period 1991–2000. This will give Mexico a population of about 99 million in 2000.

Family life: The average size of households in 1992 was 4.8. The average income per household in 1989 was $1,384. About 20 percent of people live below the poverty line, which is defined as an income of $350 per person per year. The length of holidays depends on the time at work.

Work: In 1991, the average working week in industry was 45.5 hours. The workforce in 1990 was 24,063,000. Unemployment fell from 25 percent in 1986 to 14 to17 percent in 1991.

Prices: Inflation soared in the 1980s, reaching more than 100 percent. Following economic reforms in the late 1980s, inflation fell to about 12 percent in 1992.

Religions: In 1990, Roman Catholics made up 89.7 percent of the population, Protestants 4.9 percent and people of other religions 5.4 percent.

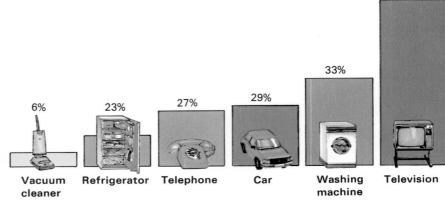

Vacuum cleaner	6%
Refrigerator	23%
Telephone	27%
Car	29%
Washing machine	33%
Television	73%

Health services	4%
Recreation	5%
Clothing and shoes	8%
Transport and communications	10%
Housing and household furnishings	23%
Food, beverages and tobacco	37%
Other goods and services	13%

△**How many households owned goods in the 1980s**
The ownership of television sets and other consumer durables is low in comparison with the United States and European countries. There has been a surge in ownership of such goods in recent years.

◁**How the average household budget was spent in 1989**
Rents in Mexico are quite low. Education and entertainment are an increasing part of family expenditure.

▽ **Mexican stamps and money**
The *peso* is divided into 100 *centavos*. Banknotes come in denominations of 100, 500, 1,000, 2,000, 5,000 and 10,000 *pesos*. There are coins of 1, 5, 10 and 50 *pesos* and also coins of 20 and 50 *centavos*.

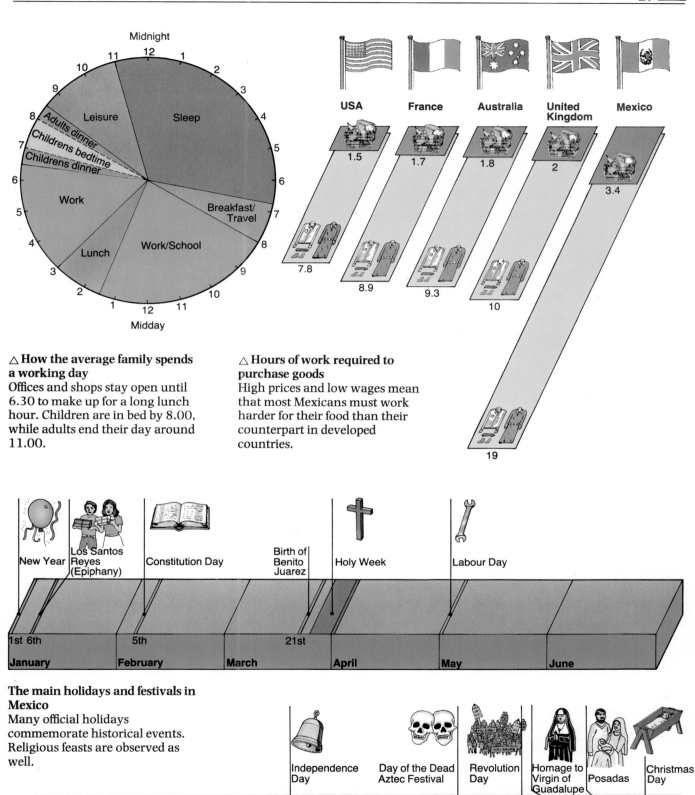

△ **How the average family spends a working day**
Offices and shops stay open until 6.30 to make up for a long lunch hour. Children are in bed by 8.00, while adults end their day around 11.00.

△ **Hours of work required to purchase goods**
High prices and low wages mean that most Mexicans must work harder for their food than their counterpart in developed countries.

USA 1.5
France 1.7
Australia 1.8
United Kingdom 2
Mexico 3.4

USA 7.8
France 8.9
Australia 9.3
United Kingdom 10
Mexico 19

The main holidays and festivals in Mexico
Many official holidays commemorate historical events. Religious feasts are observed as well.

New Year — 1st — January
Los Santos Reyes (Epiphany) — 6th — January
Constitution Day — 5th — February
Birth of Benito Juarez — 21st — March
Holy Week — April
Labour Day — May
June

Independence Day — 16th — September
Day of the Dead Aztec Festival — October
Revolution Day — 2nd, 20th — November
Homage to Virgin of Guadalupe — 12th — December
Posadas — 16–24 — December
Christmas Day — 25th — December
July
August

Farming and fishing

Only about half of Mexico is suitable for agriculture because of Mexico's dry climate and rugged mountainous terrain. In some parts of the country artificial irrigation is needed throughout the year.

Until the 19th century, most of Mexico was in the hands of a few powerful landowners. Since then there have been laws and reforms to redistribute the land. Under the *ejido* system the government owned the land, but allocated certain areas to people who worked it and then kept the profits. Because this system proved inefficient, the government introduced reforms in the early 1990s. Land can now once again be rented, sold or used as security for loans.

The main commercial farming areas are in irrigated parts of the north of the country, where cotton and wheat are the chief crops. Fruit and vegetables, such as melons and tomatoes, are grown along the fertile river valleys.

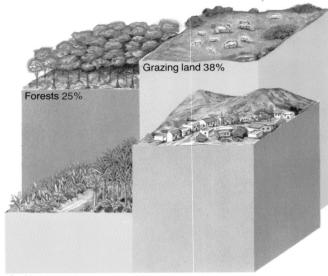

Grazing land 38%

Forests 25%

Arable land 12%   Mountains and urban 25%

Above: Land use in Mexico. The scarce arable land, where necessary, is irrigated to make it yield more crops.

Below: Ox-drawn carts, unchanged for centuries, are still a common sight in many rural areas of Mexico.

Above: Mexico grows a large amount of fruit. Apples, bananas and citrus fruits grow well along the river valleys.

Right: The blue agave plant is the source of the strong drink called *tequila*.

Below: Fishing nets on the Pacific Coast.

Mexico is one of the world's leading producers of meat. Cattle are reared in semi-arid areas in the north and sheep are grazed on the Central Plateau. The most rugged areas are suitable only for goats.

Sugar cane, coffee and fruits, including bananas, grapes, oranges and pineapples, grow on the southern plains. Cacao, the plant from which chocolate is made, is also important. The main food crop is maize (corn). It grows on nearly half of the cultivated land but, even so, Mexico still imports maize to satisfy demand.

With the introduction of refrigerated trucks, fishing has developed into a major industry. It provides employment not only for fishermen, but also for retailers and distributors who handle the catches of tuna, sardines, anchovies, squid and a variety of shellfish. The most important catches are of shrimp, many thousand tons of which are exported.

Forestry is becoming increasingly important. Most of the timber, which includes both hard and soft woods, is used for lumber.

Natural resources

Mexico's greatest asset has always been its mineral wealth. The Spanish swiftly developed the rich silver deposits of Mexico. In recent times the discovery and exploitation of oil and gas has helped the growth of Mexican industry.

Mexico was already one of the world's major oil producers in 1922, but it was the huge new reserves discovered along the gulf coast and offshore in 1976 that provided the revenues for the beginning of an industrial boom. By 1992 the country was producing 3.1 million barrels of oil a day, about one-twentieth of world production. Mexico is now the world's fifth largest oil producer. It is also a major producer of natural gas.

The many rivers that cascade down the steep valleys of the Central Plateau provide Mexico with vast amounts of hydroelectric power. Today over one-third of Mexico's energy requirements are provided by hydroelectric schemes.

Below: A large hydro-electric dam at Villahermosa. More than a third of Mexico's electricity is generated by hydro-electric plants.

Above: Oil production in Mexico is government controlled by PEMEX (Petroleos Mexicanos). Its revenues are vital to Mexico's economy.

Mexico is also endowed with a great many precious metals and other minerals that are vital to industry. The country leads the world in silver production. Mexico is also one of the world's leading producers of arsenic, bismuth, graphite, mercury and selenium.

Other important minerals include sulfur, lead, zinc, coal, uranium, iron ore, gold and copper. Much of Mexico's iron ore is used in the country's growing steel industry. Minerals are important export commodities.

In 1990, mining employed about 260,000 people. This represented 1.1 percent of the labor force.

Some of the minerals, such as coal, provide primary sources of energy while others are used to make vital components in manufacturing. The country's large cement industry gets its raw materials, sand, gravel and crushed stone, from local quarries. Mexico's large craft industry draws on the nation's vast deposits of precious metals, especially silver.

Above left: Mexico's main steel works are located at Monterrey and Monclova, close to the Sabinas coalfields.

Above: One of the richest silver mines in Mexico near Guanajuato.
Below: Tapping for resin is a profitable industry.

Industry and trade

Mexico's economy flourished during the oil boom of the 1970s, creating many new jobs. A fall in world oil prices in the 1980s led to economic crisis. Mexico's overseas debts reached high levels, while inflation and unemployment soared. From the late 1980s, the government launched reforms, including the privatization of many government-owned industries. The economy began to recover and the agreement in 1993 to set up a free trade area with Canada and the United States, called the North American Free Trade Agreement (NAFTA), encouraged the hope that Mexico would develop into a major industrial power. The United States is Mexico's most important trading partner by far.

Much of Mexico's industry is located in and around the large cities of central Mexico. Recently, however, many factories have been set up near the United States border. These industries, called *maquiladores*, assemble such products as cars, computers, electrical goods and television sets for export to the United States.

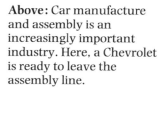

Above: Car manufacture and assembly is an increasingly important industry. Here, a Chevrolet is ready to leave the assembly line.

Left: Food processing accounts for one quarter of Mexico's industrial production, and employs half a million people. This plant is producing *tequila*.

Tourism is the second largest source of currency in Mexico. The country's rich and colorful heritage, as well as its breathtaking scenery and extensive beaches, attracted 6,600,000 visitors in 1990. One of the most famous resorts is Acapulco on the western Pacific coast, although the Caribbean coast boasts equally fine beaches with the added attractions of the Yucatán Peninsula and its Mayan ruins.

Food processing, electronics and the production of office equipment are all part of Mexico's light industry. These and other activities are closely related to the tourist industry. They include glassware, textiles, woollen goods and handicrafts. Products based on traditional designs range from gold and silver jewelry to basketware.

Other important industries in Mexico include the construction industry, which employs seven percent of the working population, and the manufacture of timber products.

Above left: An electronics plant near the US border.

Above: A tourist resort.
Below: Traditional designs are popular with tourists.

Transportation

Mexico has a modern and extensive system of highways despite the mountainous nature of the country. There are more than 29,500 miles (47,500 km) of paved macadam roads, many of which converge on Mexico City and provincial capitals, such as Guadalajara. Routes radiating from Mexico City connect the capital with other major towns and ports. Running the length of the country is the Pan American Highway, a highway system linking the United States with seventeen Latin American countries.

In 1990 the total number of motor vehicles in Mexico was nearly twelve million, of which 56 percent were cars and 44 percent were trucks. Just over 230,000 motorcycles were registered in 1990.

In the cities, buses are inexpensive and run frequently. Buses are a popular means of transport and come in all shapes and sizes, from luxury coaches with air conditioning, which are used for long journeys to old, rattling vehicles, which serve the isolated rural districts.

Above: This ferry or *panga* crosses the Grijalva River in the southern state of Tabasco. It provides an essential link for many people.

Below: A shared taxi and a bus on a highway out of Mexico City. Both are popular and inexpensive forms of transport in Mexico.

Above: An airliner from Aero-mexico's fleet at Villahermosa, in the southern part of the Gulf of Mexico.

Right: Mexico has 16,300 miles (26,300 km) of railway which has to traverse very often difficult terrain.

Air transportation has expanded greatly in recent years. By 1991 some 32 million passengers passed through Mexico's airports during the course of the year.

The main shipping ports are at Veracruz, Tampico, Coatzacoalcos, Salina Cruz, Manzanillo, Acapulco and Lázaro Cardenas. Veracruz, on the Gulf of Mexico, is the leading port. Located close by are the installations of Pajaritos, which handle most of the shipments for the petroleum industry

The railways are government run except for three small lines in private hands. The state railways receive a subsidy that makes the fares cheap and the cargo rates especially low. For this reason more cargo is moved by rail in Mexico than in many other more industrialized countries. Mexico City also has an underground system, decorated in Indian, Mexican and Spanish styles. It is as crowded during rush hours as any similar system elsewhere.

Fact file: economy and trade

	Oil and gas
	Coal
	Uranium
	Iron ore
	Silver
	Industry
	Corn
	Wheat
	Cotton
	Coffee
	Sugar cane
	Cattle
	Fishing port
	Forestry

△ **The distribution of Mexico's economic activity**
Corn, the most important crop, is grown in central and southern regions. The main industrial zones are on the Central Plateau while the largest silver mines are in the north.

Key facts

Structure of production: Of the total GDP (the value of all economic activity in Mexico), farming, forestry and fishing contribute 9 percent, industry 30 percent, and services (such as commerce and the civil service) 61 percent.
Farming: Crops are grown on about 12 percent of Mexico's land area. Grazing land makes up another 38 percent. *Main products:* cotton, coffee, fruit, wheat, sorghum, maize, sugar cane, vegetables.
Mining: In 1992, Mexico was the second largest oil producer in the Americas, after the United States. Other minerals produced in Mexico include coal, copper, gold, iron, lead, manganese, silver, sulfur, tin, uranium and zinc.
Manufacturing: Mexico has expanded its manufacturing industries greatly in the last 40 years. Major products now include chemicals, machinery, clothing, processed foods, processed petroleum and steel.
Trade (1991): Total imports: $38 billion; exports $27 billion. Mexico is the third most important trading nation in North America, after the United States and Canada.
Economic growth: The average growth rate of Mexico's gross national product between 1980–91 was 1.5 percent a year. This low rate was a reflection of the depression in the 1980s and the fall in world oil prices.

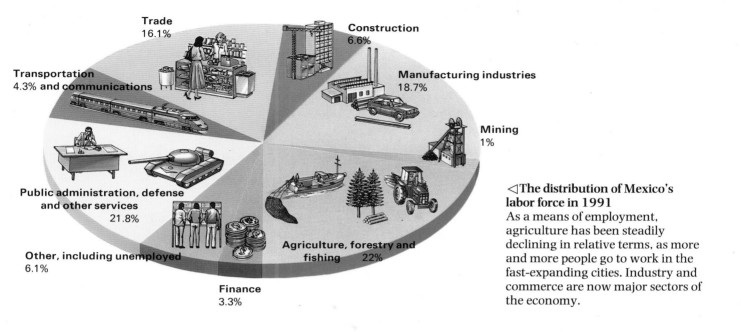

Trade 16.1%

Construction 6.6%

Transportation 4.3% **and communications**

Manufacturing industries 18.7%

Mining 1%

Public administration, defense and other services 21.8%

Other, including unemployed 6.1%

Agriculture, forestry and fishing 22%

Finance 3.3%

◁ **The distribution of Mexico's labor force in 1991**
As a means of employment, agriculture has been steadily declining in relative terms, as more and more people go to work in the fast-expanding cities. Industry and commerce are now major sectors of the economy.

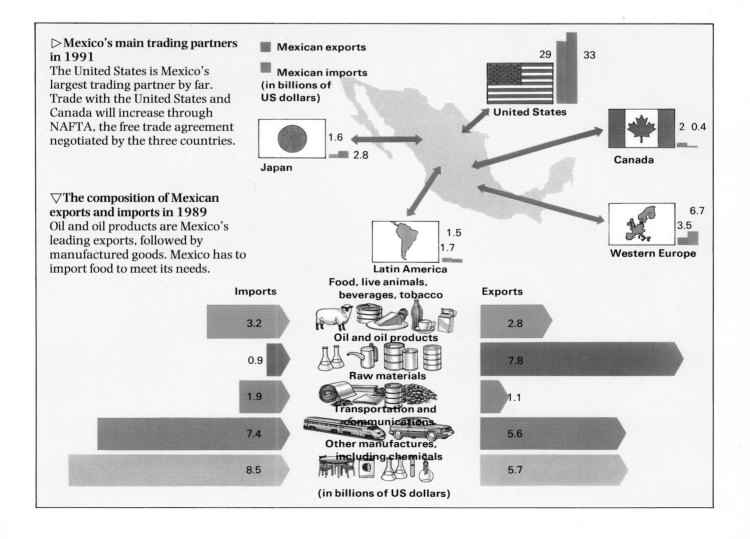

▷ **Mexico's main trading partners in 1991**
The United States is Mexico's largest trading partner by far. Trade with the United States and Canada will increase through NAFTA, the free trade agreement negotiated by the three countries.

■ Mexican exports

■ Mexican imports (in billions of US dollars)

29   33
United States

2   0.4
Canada

1.6
2.8
Japan

6.7
3.5
Western Europe

▽ **The composition of Mexican exports and imports in 1989**
Oil and oil products are Mexico's leading exports, followed by manufactured goods. Mexico has to import food to meet its needs.

1.5
1.7
Latin America

Imports   **Exports**

Food, live animals, beverages, tobacco
3.2   2.8

Oil and oil products
0.9   7.8

Raw materials
1.9   1.1

Transportation and communications
7.4   5.6

Other manufactures, including chemicals
8.5   5.7

(in billions of US dollars)

Education

Few developing countries have expanded education as vigorously as Mexico. After the 1910 Revolution, hundreds of schools were opened throughout the country. The fight for literacy gradually brought results, with a great leap forward between 1960 and 1980. By 1990, the number of people who could read and write had risen to 87 percent.

In Mexico education is compulsory and free between the ages of six and sixteen. Before the age of six, some Mexican children attend a pre-school course for two years. Primary (elementary) education lasts six years and is divided into two levels, basic and higher, each taking three years. Secondary education consists of a three-year basic curriculum, and a further three years for pupils intending to go to college.

Primary school children begin their day at 8 in the morning and finish at 1.00 p.m. Modern teaching methods are used in Mexican schools, but discipline is strict and the teacher is still a figure of respect.

Above: A primary school. Education at Mexican primary schools is free and compulsory from the age of six.

Left: The government has allocated large sums of money to build new schools and supply educational equipment for the growing population of Mexicans.

Left: Pupils using the school's computers. Many classrooms have this type of modern equipment.

Below: Students at the National University of Mexico City. A vast mosaic decorates the main library building.

Since education in Mexico is now compulsory, nearly all children are registered at a school. Mexico has achieved enrolment figures of 98 percent for children of primary school age and more than 50 percent for children of secondary school level. Even remote areas of Mexico can now receive educational broadcasts by means of a communications satellite.

Most schools in Mexico are government run. There are also many church schools that are not supported by the government. They make, however, a very valuable contribution to the educational system, especially at the secondary-school level.

More than 6,000 professional schools, including state universities, teacher training colleges and technical colleges are available for students who go on to higher education. In 1990, approximately one and a half million students were pursuing higher education. The country's oldest and largest university is in Mexico City.

The arts

The many great Indian civilizations have provided Mexico with a vast cultural treasures, including beautiful temples and impressive sculptures. Folk arts derived from ancient Indian cultures still survive. The ceramic, weaving and silverwork crafts are particularly distinguished.

But art is by no means a thing of the past in Mexico. In the early 20th century, a number of Mexican artists achieved lasting fame for their new approach to mural painting. These included José Clemente Orozco (1883–1949), David Siqueiros (1898–1974), Diego Rivera (1886–1957), and Rufino Tamayo (1899–).

Among the country's most noted composers is Carlos Chávez (1899–1978,) whose symphonic and chamber music has become part of the modern repertoire in both America and Europe. In 1952 the Mexican dancer Amalia Hernández formed the Ballet Folklórico. This dance group has two companies touring the world, and a third at the Palace of Fine Arts in Mexico City.

Above: A Mayan sculpture. Mexico's Indian heritage is the inspiration of many of its 20th-century artists.

Below: *The Time Machine* is one of Diego Rivera's colourful murals which depict social and political themes in world history.

Left: Sor Juana Inés de la Cruz, the brilliant and outspoken writer. Her prose and poetry rank among the finest of the 17th century.

Above: Octavio Paz, poet, critic and interpreter of the Mexican character.

Below: The entrance to Mexico City's Satellite Town.

But it is in literature that Mexico has, perhaps, made the greatest contribution to world culture. A long line of poets, dramatists, political writers and novelists have enriched the literature of both Spain and the New World. Among them is a 17th-century nun Sor (Sister) Juana Inés de la Cruz (1651–95), whose poetry ranks with the finest in the Spanish language. Her interest in politics and her scientific mind made her a remarkable person, far ahead of her time.

Mexico has also produced such modern writers as Juan Rulfo (1918–86), Carlos Fuentes (1928–) and Octavio Paz (1914–). Rulfo was the founder of the "magical realism" school of fiction, while Fuentes remains at the forefront of Latin American novelists. The leading writer in contemporary Mexico is the poet and essayist Octavio Paz, whose works, like those of Fuentes, have been translated into most Western languages. His writings shed great light on the Mexican personality.

The making of modern Mexico

Mexico gained independence from Spain in 1821. The new government, however, could do little to improve conditions for the common people, because the rich, landed classes still effectively ruled the country.

In 1836, north of the Rio Grande, settlers from the United States revolted against Mexican rule, and proclaimed the Republic of Texas. General López de Santa Anna rode north to the settlers' fort – an old mission called "The Poplar" (El Alamo) – and killed most of the defenders. One month later the United States army attacked and defeated the Mexican army.

In 1846 American forces stormed Mexico City. Peace came when Santa Anna, then president, ceded Texas – and later California, New Mexico and parts of Arizona – to the United States. Benito Juárez, Minister of Justice, then ordered all church and army property seized and given to the needy. Conservative groups fought these measures and a bitter civil war ensued.

Above: General López de Santa Anna, President of Mexico during the war with the United States in 1846–7.

Left: The Alamo

Below: The land acquired by the United States from Mexico during and after the Mexican War. Mexico lost half of its land area.

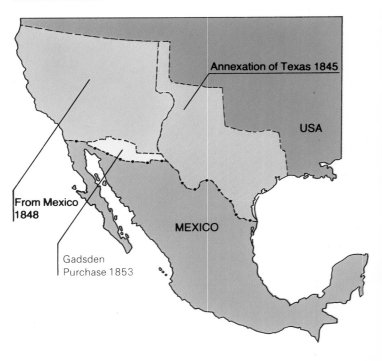

Annexation of Texas 1845

USA

From Mexico 1848

Gadsden Purchase 1853

MEXICO

Above: Archduke Maximilian of Austria is executed by firing squad in 1867. He was emperor of Mexico for only three years.

Right: Porfirio Díaz was President of Mexico for more than 30 years.
Below right: Peasants in revolt against the Díaz regime in 1910.

The war brought ruin to the economy and Juárez decided to delay payment of money owed to Spain, Britain and France. Soon all three countries landed troops to press their claims, but only the French chose to fight. Defeated initially at the Battle of Puebla (1862), France eventually routed Juárez.

In 1864 Mexican exiles, restored to power by the French, installed Archduke Maximilian of Austria as emperor. It was a short reign. Maximilian was captured in battle by Juárist forces in 1867, and promptly shot.

Under Porfirio Díaz's presidency (1876–1910), foreign investment grew. A thriving middle class also emerged, though peasants and workers still lacked the most basic human rights.

The sufferings of the poor exploded in the Mexican Revolution of 1910. It continued until the early 1930s, when socialist values became national policy. The Revolutionary Party, founded in 1929, assumed power that year and has remained in office ever since.

Mexico in the modern world

The oil boom begun in the 1970s brought enormous benefits to Mexico. It also posed a great problem – how to pay back the vast sums of money borrowed from other countries to develop a modern oil industry.

Despite the enormous strides made by Mexico, it became clear that the income produced by petroleum was not sufficient to meet repayments of the debt. Worse still, a drop in the price of oil in the 1980s meant the country's revenues were reduced. Mexico then faced a severe economic crisis.

The election of President Carlos Salinas de Gortari in 1988 led to major changes in policy. The new government began to reform agriculture by letting peasants sell or rent land that had been owned by the government. Salinas also privatized government-owned industries, encouraged foreign investment in order to create jobs, and made cutbacks in public spending. Much of the money saved was used to reduce Mexico's debts.

Above: The old and new in Mexico City. Sub-standard houses contrast sharply with modern high-rise buildings.

Left: Soccer fans at a match, during the World Cup, held in Mexico in 1986. Mexico has hosted several major events in recent years, including the Olympic Games.

Left: Rodolfo Neri, the first Mexican astronaut, went on a Space Shuttle mission in 1985. He was a crew member on a flight of the *Atlantis* shuttle.

Above: President Carlos Salinas, elected in 1988.

Below: Mexico has a vast young population. In 1990 38 percent of the people were under 15.

For many years, poor Mexicans have crossed the border into the United States in search of work. Lacking papers, few find jobs and they have been subject to arrest and detention for illegal entry. In 1992, the US border control arrested 1.2 million people attempting to enter the United States illegally. No one knows how many illegal immigrants escaped arrest. By the early 1990s, relations between the two countries were severely strained.

Despite long-standing Mexican fears of being dominated by its powerful northern neighbor, Salinas worked to improve relations with the United States. He proposed that a free trade area, established by the North American Free Trade Agreement, be negotiated by Mexico, the United States and Canada. NAFTA, which was due to be implemented in 1994, would become the world's largest and wealthiest market.

The creation of NAFTA will not stop illegal Mexican emigration. But, by creating jobs and developing Mexico's economy, it will gradually reduce the need for emigration.

Fact file: government and world role

Key facts

Official name: *Estados Unidos Mexicanos* (United Mexican States)

National flag: Three vertical stripes of green, white and red. The central white stripe bears the coat of arms, which depicts an eagle on a cactus holding a snake.

National anthem: *Mexicanos, al grito de guerra.* (Mexicans, at the war cry.)

National government: Mexico is a democratic federal republic. *Head of State:* The president, who is directly elected to a single, six-year term. The president heads the government and appoints the council of ministers and senior military and civilian officers of the state. *Congress:* The General Congress, the law-making parliament, consists of a 64-member Senate and a 500-member Chamber of Deputies. Senators serve six-year terms and deputies three-year terms.

Local government: The 31 states each have an elected governor and a Chamber of Deputies. The Federal District (Mexico City) is administered by a governor appointed by the president. The states are divided into local government areas, each with elected presidents and councils.

Defense: Enlistment into the regular army is voluntary, but for men aged 18 there is conscription into a part-time militia. *Army:* In 1991, the Army had 127,500 personnel. *Air Force:* The strength of the Air Force is about 8,000. *Navy:* The Navy had a personnel of 37,000. *Marines:* 8,000

Economic alliances: Mexico is a member of the Latin American Integration Association (LAIA), which took over from the Latin American Free Trade Association (LAFTA) in 1981. In 1992–93, Mexico negotiated the setting up of the North American Free Trade Agreement with the United States and Canada.

Political alliances: Mexico is a member of the United Nations and of the OAS (Organization of American States), which is a regional organization of the United Nations.

Members of Organization of American States (OAS)

Members of Latin American Integration Association (LAIA)

△ **Mexico in the Americas**
Mexico forms part of the Organization of American States which has its headquarters in Washington. It is also a member of the United Nations. The Latin American Integration Association (LAIA), fosters trade among the states south of the Rio Grande.

The Mexican system of government

The legislative, executive and judicial branches of the government are kept separate. The Chamber of Deputies has 500 members while the Senate has 64 – two from each state and two from the Federal District. The president has supreme executive powers and appoints the Council of Ministers. He is elected for a single six-year term by direct suffrage.

President

GOVERNMENT

Council of Ministers (Cabinet)

CONGRESS OF THE UNION (PARLIAMENT)

Chamber of Duputies

Senate

Electorate

Argentina 2,780
Australia 16,590
Canada 21,260
France 20,600
Japan 26,920
Mexico 2,870
New Zealand 12,140
Nicaragua 340
Spain 12,460
United Kingdom 16,750
United States 22,560
Venezuela 2,610

(in U.S. dollars)

△National wealth created per person in 1991

Mexico rates low in the world wealth table as compared to other developed nations. But the United Nations describes it as "a rapidly industrializing country," whose economy is changing quickly. This distinguishes it from most other developing countries.

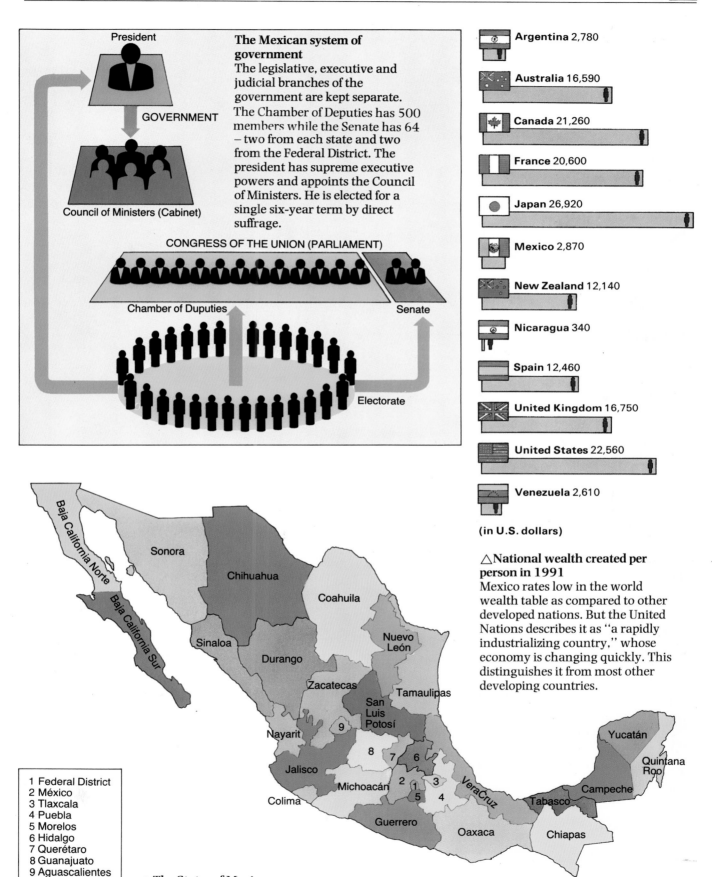

Baja California Norte
Baja California Sur
Sonora
Chihuahua
Coahuila
Sinaloa
Nuevo León
Durango
Zacatecas
Tamaulipas
San Luis Potosí
Nayarit
9
8
7
6
Jalisco
2 1 3
VeraCruz
Colima
Michoacán
5 4
Yucatán
Quintana Roo
Campeche
Tabasco
Guerrero
Oaxaca
Chiapas

1 Federal District
2 México
3 Tlaxcala
4 Puebla
5 Morelos
6 Hidalgo
7 Querétaro
8 Guanajuato
9 Aguascalientes

△ **The States of Mexico**

Index